PARENTING IS F*

London's Best Play-grounds

(to exhaust your child
and not your patience)

Written by
EMMY WATTS

HOXTON MINI PRESS

Hazel (left) aged 3, with Olive, aged 5, Victoria Park Playgrounds (p.94)

Parenting is f**king hard

...so go out and go wild in a playground

Permanent markers on the wall. Ketchup on the window. Credit cards pushed through the cracks of the floorboards. Having a family teaches you that some things are better out than in – like your child.

Fortunately, this city is a surprisingly excellent place to let miniature wild humans run amok, despite the concrete and congestion. Not only does it have great parks, but the playgrounds are also utterly fabulous too. From years of sheer desperation, we have learnt that they are brightly coloured pressure-release valves that can serve both as a destination and a passing panacea to uncork all of that bonkers but wondrous energy your children build up. The trouble is knowing which of the thousands on offer are actually worth visiting. Emmy, our brilliant writer, has been our guide and together we have made this book – the book we longed for when we first had our kids and wanted them to swing on some monkey bars rather than turning our home (and minds) upside down.

Martin & Ann, with Olive & Hazel

Royal Air Force Museum (p.38)
Opposite: Spring Park (p.54)

Claremont Park (p.46)

Best For...

Grand days out

Hampton Court's myths-and-legends-themed Magic Garden (p.112) playground is practically a full day out on its own. Add in a romp through the palace and meander through the maze and you've got yourself a positively epic adventure. Or head to Hobbledown Heath (p.116), a mystical land of enchanting animals and imaginative out-door playscapes.

Meeting non-parent friends

Highgate Wood's (p.48) scenic location and nearby cafe make it the perfect middle ground for child-free mates and chill-free little monsters. Or grab a couple of coffees from one of Exmouth Market's many stylish cafes and head to Spa Fields' (p.22) picturesque play area for a catch-up while they frolic.

Adventurous big kids

With its perplexing labyrinths, towering timber structures and ample clambering opportunities, Three Corners (p.14) is a dream come true for older ones, who can even be dropped off to explore independently. Or try Cator Park North (p.110), whose lofty nest structures and twisting tube slides mean it's absolutely not for the faint-hearted.

Mixed ages

It's rare to find a playground that caters to toddlers through to teens, but Paddington Recreation Ground (p.140) is the ultimate example, with two beautifully designed spaces cunningly connected via a bridge. Or head to Coram's Fields (p.26), a kids-only park with enough play areas to keep everyone happy.

Tiny toddlers

Marvellous Maze's (p.80) pint-sized playground is ideal for under-5s with its low-walled labyrinth and sensory features including talking tubes, musical instruments and tactile surfaces. Meanwhile, in Bloomsbury, Alf Barrett Playground (p.18) offers loads for little ones, from baby swings to gentle clambering, all reassuringly encircled by a toddler-proof gate.

Design-conscious parents

When you spend such a large chunk of your life in playgrounds, you might as well pick one that's aesthetically pleasing. The Golden Lane Estate's (p.20) architect-designed play space more than fits the bill with its muted palette and multilevel concrete rockery, while the Clapham Park Estate's (p.132) spiralling 1960s slide structure is a must-visit for Brutalism buffs.

Sweltering summers

When the temperature rises, head to one of the capital's revitalising splash pads in search of squelchy fun. Favourite fountains include Elephant Springs' (p.102) natural waterscape play area, Victoria Park's (p.94) spiralling concrete splash pool, and Tumbling Bay's (p.90) enticing jumble of dams, streams and water pumps. Super-soakers optional.

Accessibility

Gloucester Gate's playground (p.36) was designed with inclusivity in mind, with a wheelchair-accessible roundabout and ramp, plus raised tables for water play. Similarly, Greenwich Park Playground (p.106) was devised with input from parents of disabled children, and features a widened slide, thoughtfully placed paths and plenty of sensory elements.

Parent hard, play harder

Playgrounds are the unifying backdrops to our childhoods. If we were all given a pen and asked to jot down the first three playground memories that sprung to mind, they'd probably all be roughly comparable. Who could forget that first lightly chlorinated whiff of a freshly filled paddling pool, or the thrill – and ensuing nausea – of a big kid pushing us too fast on the roundabout? We'd recall the raw ecstasy of stumbling across an incredible new one. The comfort of an old faithful. The friends we made. The risks we took. The scars we earned.

In a world (and city) that isn't built for children, playgrounds provide vital havens for them to not just play, but to relax, collaborate, experiment and simply be allowed to be young. In London, where the population of under-16s is nearly two million but living space is at an obscene premium and decent-sized gardens are practically mythical, playgrounds offer an indispensable public good.

In spite of all this, the capital's playground history is woefully short. Just a century ago, London had less than 50 dedicated public play spaces, with the majority taking the form of outdoor gymnasiums designed for structured exercise rather than incubators of juvenile joy. But in the 1940s, a bombed-out London gave rise to a new breed of playground. Inspired by young Londoners creating playscapes from the rubble, the pioneering adventure playground factored in scrap materials and other loose parts, offering children the opportunity to dream up their own wildly imaginative play equipment, free from adult intervention. By the 1970s, around 100 of these experimental 'junk' playgrounds had popped up across the city, along with hundreds of more conventional fixed-equipment offerings – though now with the workout equipment traded for the ubiquitous witch's hat and iconic multi-seater rocking horse.

Today, London is home to a dizzying number of children's playgrounds, some positively spectacular and some admittedly less so, with the play provision in a fair few boroughs still seriously lacking. I've spent the last seven years seeking out the best playgrounds from all across the capital, while my kids have been given the incredibly tough job of testing them out. And while you might assume we'd found the formula for the perfect playground somewhere along the way, we haven't. Even the designers seem to be scratching their collective heads when it comes to what makes the ultimate play space. Maybe that's because there's simply no such thing. Take, for example, Elephant Park's gorgeously landscaped, summer-ready splash pool (p.102) – by no means an exhaustive playground but an incredible setting for a hot summer's day. Or muf's concrete-slabbed Golden Lane Estate play area (p.20) – tiny, but with inventive features that make it the perfect way to kill 30 minutes in the City. Maybe, just maybe, variety is the very thing kids need.

And what about us grown-ups? Surely we need variety too? We spend such a large chunk of our lives in these places, we might as well enjoy a sanity-preserving change of scenery while we're there. And then there's the endless bribery potential. Playgrounds are an excellent bargaining tool. Your offspring might not give a hoot about that new art exhibition you want to see on the other side of town, but the promise of swinging by a great playground afterwards might be all the motivation they need – particularly if it's one they've yet to explore.

Some of these playgrounds are simply so great they must be seen to be believed, even if it means a disproportionately long ride on the

District Line (trust me, it's a small price to pay). With the exception of a couple of remarkably ancient slides, most are a million miles more impressive than anything the vast majority of us will have experienced in our youths, which might be profoundly unjust, but at least we can enjoy them vicariously through our kids. In fact, never mind vicariously. I'll see you on the zip wire.

Emmy Watts (aged 2½, 1989),
London

Three Corners

Adventurous play for little thrill-seekers

A brilliant central location? *Check.* Varied equipment? *Check.* Unfettered fun for all ages? *Check.* Three Corners is everything you could possibly want in an adventure playground and then some, offering a play experience like you've never seen before – that is, unless you've previously encountered a huge vertical labyrinth spun from red netting, or a mirror maze housed in a towering timber castle. There are more traditional features too, from inward-facing swings to a curly tube slide and that most ubiquitous of adventure playground apparatus – a zip wire, but this is still very far from your average playtime. Families with under-6s are allowed just two hours a week to get their Three Corners fix, though with such vertiginous structures it's really better suited to older kids, who can be dropped off for a longer play while you indulge in an idle mooch on neighbouring Exmouth Market.

NEARBY

Exmouth Market has it all, from cool cafes to browsable boutiques. Islington Museum's abundant interactives make the area's fascinating past palatable to even the tiniest historians, and the Postal Museum's themed play area and Mail Rail ride are always a hit.

DETAILS

Facilities: Toilets
Address: Northampton Road, EC1R 0HU
Station: Farringdon

Alf Barrett Playground

Scamper along the spine of a giant lizard

This pocket park recently underwent a magical transformation, turning one of the saddest spots in central London into an inventive fairytale playscape helmed by a gigantic lizard. Aimed at under-eights, the playground might be small, but its ingenious new design offers virtually limitless play potential, with rolling hills to scale, clandestine tunnels to slither through, stepping stones to navigate and an elevated platform to occupy, making it the perfect base for classic playground games as well as more inventive play. Designed to be more inclusive than its predecessor, the playground also boasts a wheelchair-friendly design, complete with accessible roundabout and wide slide. Keep an eye out for the sculpture of Humphry, the ginger tomcat who once prowled the park.

NEARBY

The neighbouring October Gallery runs brilliant family art sessions on the last Saturday of the month. Other local amusements include eccentric gaming arcade Novelty Automation and buzzy bowling alley and diner All Star Lanes.

DETAILS

Address: 32 Old Gloucester Street, WC1N 3AD
Station: Holborn

Golden Lane Estate

Small but perfectly formed play space

It's *technically* reserved for the young residents of Chamberlin, Powell and Bon's Grade II-listed estate, but it's hard to resist a romp around this contemporary pocket playground – especially when you consider the area's lack of decent public playgrounds. Designed by landscape architects muf, with plenty of imaginative input from local schoolkids, this sunken site might be hard to locate but it's a delight once you do, with inventive multifunctional play furniture and a soothing neutral aesthetic that might make you want to hang out there longer than you'd intended. A tiny stage, ample seating, a retro-style climbing frame and even a secret slide have all been cunningly crammed into this elliptical plot, while its tightly stacked slabs of natural stone offer boundless bouldering opportunities (and its thick concrete periphery will securely contain runaway toddlers).

NEARBY

Head to h.o.m.e on Goswell Road for great coffee and healthy lunches. The Barbican Centre's popular Squish Space sessions offer a sensory smorgasbord for under-5s, while its conservatory is a verdant indoor oasis in the heart of the City.

DETAILS

Address: Golden Lane, EC1Y 0RD
Station: Barbican

Spa Fields

Fantasy playscape dreamt up by kids

Aliens exist. At least, that's what this otherworldly playground might have you believe. Here, strange UFO-like structures rest on a carpet of mysterious mounds, as if ready to take off. Believe it or not, its design is not the work of extra-terrestrials but a bunch of local schoolkids hankering for a fantastical, age-inclusive place to meet and play. In this imagined world, tightropes bridge gaping hollows, wonky steps pave the way up to spike-topped forts, and chairs perch atop 6ft ladders like the thrones of leggy overlords. While the taller structures are more accessible to toddlers than you might hope (and rain makes those mounds heart-stoppingly treacherous), it's still a top spot to take younger kids, with fanciful looks and a wonderfully non-prescriptive design that make it the ultimate backdrop for imaginative play.

NEARBY

For coffee, try Caravan on Exmouth Market. The Postal Museum is perfect for younger children with its abundant interactives and cute play space, while Islington Museum presents the area's fascinating history in a fun, hands-on way.

DETAILS

Address: Skinner Street, EC1R 0WX

Station: Angel

Coram's Fields

Historic kids-only park

Its playgrounds might not be anything particularly pioneering, but Coram's Fields has been a trailblazer for children's rights for nearly three centuries. Established as London's first public playground in 1936, the 12-acre park was once the site of philanthropist Thomas Coram's Foundling Hospital for abandoned children, and remains devoted to kids to this day, being the only green space in London to refuse entry to adults who aren't accompanied by one. Equipment ranges from toddler-ready sand-play structures in cheerful primary hues to a majestic treehouse tower and climbing wall for big kids, with wooden multi-play equipment bridging the gap between the two. Most areas feel ripe for a revamp, from the now-defunct petting zoo to the pint-sized loos, but luckily the site's magic transcends its tiredness, conserving its status as one of the capital's most treasured parks.

NEARBY

The Foundling Museum tells the heart-rending story of the former hospital and hosts brilliant workshops in school holidays, while the Charles Dickens Museum runs dedicated tours for families. For coffee (and cinnamon buns), head to Redemption Roasters on Lamb's Conduit Street.

DETAILS

Facilities: Toilets, cafe, picnic benches
Address: 93 Guildford Street, WC1N 1DN
Station: Russell Square

Stationers Park

Tolkienesque towers and a toddler park too

With its ramshackle aesthetic, all fantasy turrets and stilted walkways, this small but well-loved park's fairy-tale fortress – perched atop a perpetually muddy hill – is one of north London's most easily recognisable climbing frames, boasting rickety bridges, treacherous entry points and snaking slides that make for some properly adventurous play. Alongside timber teepees and tyre swings, there's also a gentler (though still extremely popular) play area that's perfect for under-5s. Here, smaller explorers can navigate an assortment of newly installed structures, from Wendy houses to ever-present bouncers. Start your visit at the cafe kiosk on the park's north side, where you can raid the well-stocked toy chest and fuel up on chocolate banana bread before hitting the swings.

NEARBY

The trains that once chugged along the route of the Parkland Walk may be long gone, but its verdant paths will have you feeling like you've boarded one right out of London. For toys and kidswear, you can't beat Niddle Noddle with its in-store helter skelter.

DETAILS

Facilities: Toilets, baby change, cafe, picnic benches
Address: Mayfield Road, N8 9LP
Station: Harringay

Alexandra Road Park

Inventive playgrounds on a Brutalist estate

There are many reasons to visit this curious Camden green space, and its quirky playgrounds are only three of them. Originally constructed for the young residents of the surrounding Alexandra and Ainsworth estate – a Brutalist masterpiece that's served as the backdrop to many a noirish TV show – the park underwent an award-winning redesign by playground masters Erect Architecture in 2015 that combines elements of the original design with modern equipment. Taking the form of a series of walled outdoor 'rooms', there's a visually striking red swing area, a spectacular yellow climbing frame recommended for ages 6+ and a more traditional, though still pleasingly odd, wood-dominated playground aimed at under-5s. Bring a ball and make use of the fourth 'room', a recessed multi-pitch area, while you're there.

NEARBY

Grab a strong pre-playground coffee from Liten on Fairhazel Gardens. Later, recreate The Beatles' iconic album cover over on Abbey Road before heading for a scenic stroll on Primrose Hill, or try The Sherriff Centre for soft play and good hot chocolate.

DETAILS

Address: Langtry Walk, NW8 0DU
Station: South Hampstead

Gloucester Gate

Natural and inclusive playscape in Regent's Park

Regent's Park's most northerly playground was renovated in 2020, when environmental planners LUC magicked a rather stark 1980s arrangement of turreted slides and retro roundabouts into a dreamily landscaped natural playground. Designed as a fully inclusive space with meandering wheelchair-ready ramps and accessible swings and roundabouts, the new Gloucester Gate is wildly popular with local (and not-so-local) kids all year round, even hosting an occasional Play in the Park loose parts session that's completely free of charge. And with its plant-heavy (and adult-pacifying) good looks, teen-gratifying zip wire and toddler-pleasing sand and water play area – not to mention the myriad seating options for jaded parent/carer perching – it bridges age brackets as much as it does abilities. Head here in good weather with buckets and spades, or in bad with wellies and puddle suits – it's perfect whatever the season.

NEARBY

ZSL London Zoo is within spitting distance of the playground, and both Camden Town's famous markets and Notting Hill's boutiques are just a few minutes' walk away. Get your caffeine fix en route from The Broad Walk's Espresso Bar.

DETAILS

Facilities: Toilets, baby change, cafe, picnic benches
Address: 11 Gloucester Gate, NW1 4HG
Station: Camden Town

Royal Air Force Museum

Mini aviators get ready to take-off

Young aviation fans will be flying high when they spy this fabulous themed playground, which draws inspiration from the RAF Museum's vast assortment of military aircraft. What the space lacks in square footage, it makes up for with its generous array of unique apparatus, including a hovering yellow rescue helicopter for clambering, a double Concorde slide and replica Spitfire, plus a scaled-down version of the site's Grahame-White Watchtower that's perfect for hide and seek. Access the playground via the main museum where entry is free for all and the exhibits are seriously underrated, spanning six hangars (it occupies the site of the former Hendon Aerodrome) full of aircraft and interactives. Time pre-schooler visits to coincide with the museum's Little Swifts craft and singing sessions – every second Tuesday and last Thursday of the month.

NEARBY

Exploring the museum's many hangars will easily fill a day, but if you'd prefer to move on then the brightly coloured, bouncy nirvana that is Inflata Nation is just a short walk away.

DETAILS

Facilities: Toilets, baby change, cafe, picnic benches
Address: Grahame Park Way, NW9 5LL
Station: Colindale

Kilburn Grange Park

Nature-inspired playscape in a former arboretum

Rising from the ashes of the iconic adventure playground that once occupied this leafy site – a victim of funding cuts that have spelled the end for many of its kind – the new adventure playground might lack playworkers and loose parts but it certainly lives up to its name, offering kids of all ages (the sign on the gate designates it for 0–14s) the chance to boldly play in a way that many more prescriptive playgrounds don't allow. The main event here is a visually stunning yet seemingly haphazard arrangement of logs that echoes the surrounding trees and references the site's former life as a Victorian arboretum, combining nest-like hideaways with treetop rope tunnels, precarious walkways, and a high-speed tunnel slide. Elsewhere, find water play, a standing seesaw and unusually long-chained swings that make for a seriously thrilling ride.

NEARBY

Head to Wired Co. on Broadhurst Gardens for doorstop sandwiches and Climpson coffee. Should the weather take a turn, seek sanctuary in the Sherriff Centre's three-storey soft play and friendly cafe – all housed in a stunning Victorian church.

DETAILS

Address: Kingsgate Road, NW6 2JG
Station: Brondesbury

Marylebone Green

Arty playground with a fun folly

Unlike neighbouring Gloucester Gate, which seems to blend effortlessly into the natural environs of Regent's Park, this unusual playground feels at odds with its surroundings – namely the park's neatly manicured English Gardens – with an imposing concrete folly as its centrepiece. There's a good reason for that though: the folly's design draws inspiration from Frieze, the illustrious art fair that pops up in the park every year, making it no stranger to outlandish structures. Perched on the edge of a huge sandpit and water-play area, the folly houses a big half-covered slide, climbing wall and 'secret' room equipped with a large xylophone. Elsewhere in the space you'll find all the usual suspects – a roundabout, fort-style climber and a few sets of swings – plus a 'natural' play area with logs and tunnels. Head here during Frieze Sculpture season for an added dose of culture.

NEARBY

Wander south down Marylebone High Street for all the indie shops and cosy pubs you could desire, ending up at the family-friendly (and free) Wallace Collection.

DETAILS

Facilities: Toilets, baby change, cafe, picnic benches
Address: Regent's Park, Chester Road, NW1 4NR
Station: Regent's Park

Claremont Park

Exciting inclusive play in biodiverse surrounds

It might be rather inelegantly sandwiched between the A41, North Circular and the Midland Main Line, but that doesn't make this capacious playground any less impressive. Designed for all ages and abilities, this newly opened playscape is equipped with wheelchair-accessible surfaces and apparatus; sensory elements including musical instruments and diverse textures; and equipment that will challenge even long-legged teens – an age group that's woefully under-served by most playgrounds. Clever landscaping ups the enjoyment factor, with stone climbing walls, a natural water-play area with slopes and dams, and a strong visual cohesion with the wider park, whose varied plant life has been selected to promote biodiversity. The presence of an on-site food and drink kiosk makes staying all day a real possibility – just take a seat on one of the many benches and enjoy.

NEARBY

Jewish bakery and Hampstead institution Karma Bread has an outpost on the edge of the park, alongside Neapolitan pizzeria Happy Face. Kids still got some unspent energy? Head for the springy delights of the Flip Out Trampoline Park.

DETAILS

Facilities: Toilets, baby change, cafe, picnic benches
Address: Claremont Way, Brent Cross, NW2 1AJ
Station: Brent Cross

Highgate Wood Playground

Retro fun in an ancient forest

Its equipment may be as antiquated as the woodland that surrounds it (or, at least, it seems that way), but that doesn't make this iconic playground any less worth a visit. In fact, its nostalgic delights are all part of its quirky charm, with fan favourites including wobbly 1990s ride-on vehicles, a step-mounted plastic tunnel slide and copious climbing frames in varied shapes and sizes. So large it warrants its own (endearingly idiosyncratic) map, this shady spot will keep youngsters of all ages occupied for the best part of a day, across two separate areas – one for under-5s and one for under-12s – while their adults observe from one of the many benches. Head here after your Sunday stroll, then sate their post-playground appetites with kids' comfort classics from the neighbouring Pavilion Cafe, run by falafel aficionados Hoxton Beach.

NEARBY

Schedule a stop at The Grocery Post for coffee, pastries and a bottle of organic wine for later. Or why not coincide your trip with a visit to Jacksons Lane for lively kids' classes and pioneering theatre the entire family will enjoy?

DETAILS

Facilities: Toilets, baby change, cafe, picnic benches
Address: Muswell Hill Road, N10 3JN
Station: Highgate

Astey's Row

Quirky climbing in a brightly coloured boulderscape

London's most colourful playground is also probably its narrowest, occupying a curious, snake-shaped plot behind Essex Road station that makes very little sense until you realise that it was once a 17th-century waterway. The playground's awkward shape has no bearing on its fun factor, however, with an interesting array of apparatus – both conventional and more imaginative – on offer. Older kids are well catered for here, courtesy of a wobbly-rope climbing frame, balance-log assault course and a pair of somewhat precarious slides, while younger ones will appreciate the water pump-equipped sandpit and highlighter-bright boulders of varying heights for scramblers of all sizes. The wonderfully overgrown rock garden at the playground's western edge extends the playable space, while the New River Walk, just across the road, is a top spot for nature observation and provides welcome relief from the pandemonium of the playground.

NEARBY

Pop to Popham's for the area's best coffee and croissants, Molly-Meg for dreamy kids' homeware and gifts, Little Angel for magical children's theatre and Maggie & Rose cafe for light lunches in a kid-friendly space.

DETAILS

Address: Canonbury Villas, N1 2HE
Station: Essex Road

Spring Park

Enormous playscape in beautiful surrounds

Despite being built as part of the regeneration of Woodberry Down, Spring Park's appeal extends far beyond even this vast development. Perched on the edge of the picturesque Woodberry Wetlands and serene New River Walk, it's the ideal stop-off for scenic family strolls, as well as offering one of the capital's most spectacular playground backdrops – something that's more important than you'd think. Equipment varies from a toddler-ready multi-play frame to a lofty pyramid tower that bigger kids can launch themselves from by way of a gargantuan tube slide, as well as a climbing wall, multiple balance apparatus and a ping-pong table. Best of all, the playable space is massive, spanning acres of beautifully landscaped terrain with not a single car in sight.

NEARBY

Grab a coffee en route from Woodberry Wetlands' Coal House Cafe, or head down post-play for a refuel. Climbing wall whet their appetite? Give them a real challenge at The Castle Climbing Centre. Or head to Abney Park Cemetery for some faded grandeur.

DETAILS

Address: 6 Town Court Path, Woodberry Down, N4 2TJ
Station: Manor House

Highbury Fields

Old-school fun for all

If ever a playground had it all, it's this eclectic gem in Islington's largest park. An exhilarating patchwork of diverse equipment, Highbury Fields truly offers something for everyone, from an enormous sandpit scattered with toddler equipment to a stimulating big kids' zone boasting towering pyramids, a soaring zip wire and a flame-hued wooden climber. Well-loved – but still fully functional – retro apparatus include an excellent pedal-powered roundabout and one of the best examples of a mound slide you'll likely ever encounter, while the recently refurbished splash pad is a powerful kid magnet come summer. And if that's still not enough to placate twitchy toddlers, the park's popular 'toy graveyard' is bound to keep them busy with its motley collection of plastic Wendy houses and Cozy Coupes in various states of love-worn decay.

NEARBY

Indie kids' design store Molly Meg, the Little Angel puppet theatre and Maggie & Rose's cosy play cafe are all within walking distance. For a matcha latte, head to Kissa Wa Cafe on the adjacent Corsica Street.

DETAILS

Facilities: Toilets, picnic benches
Address: 8 Highbury Crescent, N5 1RN
Station: Highbury & Islington

Barnard Adventure Playground

Towering fun among the treetops

With its sweeping walkways, lofty treehouse dens and access routes that will scare the living daylights out of even the most permissive parents, this sprawling playground on stilts is definitely not for the faint hearted, but confident climbers will adore it. Barnard playfully references its history as one of the oldest adventure playgrounds in Islington with traditional wood structures based on the (sadly long gone) 1970s originals. Speeding zip wires, a large climbing wall and a little amphitheatre where kids can stage plays or whoosh down a ramp on battered ride-ons are just some of the treats that lie in store for young visitors. Like all adventure playgrounds in the borough, Barnard limits its open-access hours for families to 11.30am–1.30pm on a Saturday, but this should provide more than enough time to tire out tinies – not to mention their adults.

NEARBY

Grab your pre-playground coffee and snacks from neighbouring organic store Healthy-ish. Afterwards, head to nearby kid-friendly cafes Poppets Stores or Maggie & Rose for pastries and play, or to Little Angel Theatre for inspiring puppetry for kids of all ages.

DETAILS

Facilities: Toilets
Address: Copenhagen Street, N1 0FB
Station: Angel

Hornsey Park

Creative climbing with a super-fast slide

Built to serve the residents of Haringey's new Clarendon Gasworks, this small but interesting spot has managed to fill a gaping void in the area's play provision, expanding its appeal far beyond the estate's edge. Where many playground designs feel chaotic, this feels considered, with equipment limited to three key structures, each offering endless scope for play. A honeycomb-like arrangement of dens caters to smaller explorers, while a sprawling concrete rope course featuring climbing webs, hammocks and colourful foot holds accommodates bigger kids. At the front of the space, a lofty octagonal tower commands a hillside position that allows for an extra-long slide and makes for a thrilling ride back down to earth. Meanwhile, the row of wooden sun loungers offers a welcome treat for flagging adults come the summer months, even if they seem a weirdly optimistic addition for the remainder of the year.

NEARBY

There's no shortage of gaudy soft plays in this part of town but Little Dinosaurs is the best. Supposing you're after something more adult-friendly, head to The Goodness Brewing Company for pints, pizza and bouncy-castle joy.

DETAILS

Address: Hornsey Park Road, N8 0JX
Station: Hornsey, Turnpike Lane

Somerford Grove

Colourful, community-focused space

Tucked in the shadow of the Spurs' Stadium, Somerford is a community-led adventure playground that is mostly populated by the local kids who helped build it. It is a magical space that oozes community spirit without ever feeling exclusive. On Saturdays, the playground opens its doors to children of all ages, albeit with grown-ups required to accompany under-6s for the duration, while its after-school provision for older kids includes a weekly SisterHood Project session that's specially reserved for girls. Like with many spaces of its kind, the playground is constantly evolving, with inventive new structures seemingly popping up with every visit. Vibrant greenhouses perch atop mature trees, an elliptical den offers shelter as well as climbing opportunities thanks to a well-placed platform, and a multi-storey tower provides endless scope for clambering and (cushioned) jumping. One you'll be heading back to again and again (whether you like it or not).

NEARBY

Roller Nation runs a relaxed Family Jam roller disco every Saturday, while Bruce Castle Museum offers a dedicated family gallery filled with toys and interactives. Beavertown's family-friendly Corner Pin Pub, meanwhile, offers the ideal spot for a post-romp pint.

DETAILS

Facilities: Toilets
Address: Park Lane Close, N17 0HL
Station: Northumberland Park

Queen's Park

Large and leafy play park with a city farm

While not ground-breaking as far as its equipment goes, Queen's Park offers a pretty excellent playground by most kids' standards. This popular spot comprises a spacious big kids' area that will challenge adventurers well into their teens with its looming pyramid slide, giant log jumble and rocketing zip wire; while its well-secured under-5s zone invites little ones to independently explore a sandy settlement of charmingly retro playhouses and vehicles. Surprisingly few people seem to be aware of the tiny children's farm that's home to goats, sheep, ducks and turkeys on the other side of the park, but the paddling pool commands a great deal of attention come the summer months. Follow the crowd and head here on a baking hot day armed with buckets, spades and plenty of snacks.

NEARBY

Mini Picassos' creative classes draw inspiration from the work of famous artists and cater to all, from toddlers to adults. Or try Sammy's Soft Play, Yogaloft's oddly serene indoor playground boasting comfy sofas and an excellent vegetarian cafe.

DETAILS

Facilities: Toilets, baby change, cafe, picnic benches
Address: Kingswood Avenue, NW6 6EN
Station: Queen's Park

Parsloes Park

Multicolour designer playscape

It's not often a council commissions artists to design their playgrounds, and when they do, the resulting spaces are usually criticised for prioritising style over play value. While that might be the case for at least one of this Dagenham park's eye-catching new playgrounds, devised by London-based artists Eva Rothschild and Yinka Ilori to replace their long-dilapidated predecessors, it's hard to refute the joy of their respective colour palettes or the quirkiness of their forms. Rothschild's Parsloes Memphis playground consists of three brightly hued steel pyramids – a dream for leggy older kids and teens; while Ilori's Flamboyance of Flamingos is better suited to younger tots, referencing the artist's Nigerian heritage as well as the park's feathered former residents with its colour scheme, flamingo bouncers and nest-shaped slide. Admittedly there are limited opportunities for challenging play here, but it sure is pretty.

NEARBY

Barking Sportshouse and Gym in nearby Mayesbrook Park is home to a massive trampoline park and soft play that kids will lose their minds over.

DETAILS

Address: Ivy Walk, RM9 5RX
Station: Becontree

West Ham Park

It's playtime ahoy for little explorers

In 2022 this leafy park's tired but well-loved playground underwent its biggest revamp in 35 years, in a move that saw its mismatched patchwork of faded metal apparatus replaced by a much more cohesive scheme themed around the park's botanical history. Invitingly scalable organic play sculptures, extensive water features and an abundance of sustainable timber and stone make the new design a much more attractive play prospect for kids – not to mention a more inviting backdrop for their adults. At the centre, an interpretation of explorer John Fothergill's ship the Endeavour nods to the physician and plant collector's role in the establishment of the park, while providing endless imaginative-play opportunities for all ages. Don't miss the site's most treasured possession – a pair of retro monkey swings that, despite losing their swing function, retain every ounce of their 1980s charm.

NEARBY

Stratford's Discover Children's Story Centre offers three floors of immersive play plus an imaginative Story Garden. Alternatively, head to Forest Gate for pub grub and miniature railway rides at The Holly Tree, or coffee and playtime at The Can Club.

DETAILS

Facilities: Toilets, cafe, picnic benches
Address: Upton Lane, E7 9PU
Station: Plaistow

Biodiversity Playground

Fairy-tale fun to feed little imaginations

Danish playground designer Monstrum has successfully created one of the capital's most magnificent playscapes on what might otherwise have been a rather uninspiring site, unceremoniously wedged between a mainline rail station and a shopping mall. Drawing inspiration from the work of folklore master Hans Christian Andersen, this magical play area is notable for its imaginative themed structures – all beautifully made using sustainable timber and finished in Monstrum's signature palette of vibrant hues. Bubble gum-pink lily pad bouncers, sloping white origami boats, ornamental bridges, a leaf-green frog slide and an enormous flame-hued, hollow-bellied carp float on a sea of blue and green spongy surfacing offers a welcome break from the monotony of traditional playground design – not to mention the madness of Westfield on a weekend.

NEARBY

Supposing you're not here for the shops, head north to the East Village for good coffee and Greek eats from Hand, or velvety gelato from La Gelateria. Kids will love the mirror maze installation, as well as the dozen or so more playgrounds dotted around the area.

DETAILS

Facilities: Toilets, baby change, cafe
Address: Westfield Stratford City, E20 1EJ
Station: Stratford International

Sunrise Close Play Area

Distinctive design-conscious playscape for all ages

From Rietveld's chairs to van Eyck's playgrounds, the Dutch are famed for their visionary design. Amsterdam-based landscape architects Carve might not be *quite* so illustrious, but their East Village playscape is certainly unique, having been designed to mimic the triangular geometry of the surrounding apartment blocks. Children of all ages are well catered for here, with both big and little kids' areas separated by spurting play fountains that will be popular with both. On the under-5s side, tangerine-hued pods conceal tiny swings, rope ladders and hidden slides. For older ones, a large cluster of modular play crystals forms a maze suspended on stilts, providing infinite possibilities as well as a pleasing visual contrast in a rich shade of grey-blue. Granted, this part of east London is no stranger to unusual playgrounds, but supposing you're stuck for which to choose, be sure to go Dutch.

NEARBY

Neighbouring Bakehouse by Signorelli is ideal for a post-play refuel and also runs popular Little Bakers sessions, offering younger kids the chance to decorate their own cupcakes over a babyccino.

DETAILS

Address: Sunrise Close, E20 1DU

Station: Stratford International

Marvellous Maze

Sensory fun for younger kids

While by no means a 'destination' playground, this small but very sweet quayside diversion is the ideal place to deposit toddlers, who'll lap up its adorable arrangement of Lilliputian bridges, perplexing paths and tiny tunnels while their grown-ups admire the river view. And while the site might be pint-sized, designer Erect Architecture's magical mirror-maze design actually makes it feel significantly bigger, multi-sensory elements including musical instruments, talking tubes and tactile installations will keep little ones occupied for longer than you'd think. Still not satisfied? Check out neighbouring Harbord Square Park's equally diminutive under-5s play area for virtually endless sand and water fun featuring easy-to-push hand pumps and a dam system designed to encourage collaborative play. Family trips to Canary Wharf just got that (tiny) bit easier.

NEARBY

The interactive Mudlarks gallery at the Museum of London Docklands boasts transport-themed soft play along with many other child-friendly delights. Worked up an appetite? Mercato Metropolitano and Dishoom are both perfect for families.

DETAILS

Address: Harbour Quay Gardens, E14 5FW
Station: Canary Wharf

All Mead Gardens

Eccentric estate playground with a fishy folly

A surprise awaits curious kids at Hackney's Kingsmead Estate. Tucked between the red-brick blocks, this unusual space might officially be called All Mead Gardens, but to local children it's the Fish Playground, named for the huge concrete fish head that forms its unlikely centrepiece and functions as a clubhouse, hidey-hole and rain shelter, among countless other possibilities. Directly opposite, what could feasibly be London's most precarious slide adds to All Mead's list of oddities, accessed via a long ladder, and completely uncovered despite its elevation and sharp twists and turns, while behind that an equally lengthy (but much less lofty) hillside slide provides a less terrifying alternative. Next door in the under-5s playground things are equally unconventional, with fish-shaped bouncers and stone sculptures orbited by colourful tarmac, and a network of peekaboo-perfect wooden walls. A must if you're in the area with kids.

NEARBY

The many foodie delights of Chatsworth Road are just a 10-minute walk away. A Small Triangle is the place for stylish children's gifts (or its parent store, Triangle, for seriously chic womenswear), and if you're in the mood for a cultural treat then head to Chats Palace for family theatre.

DETAILS

Address: Kingsmead Estate, E9 5QN
Station: Homerton

Forrester Way

Pocket park with a mammoth play tower

Stratford is now home to a glorious number of playgrounds, thanks to a policy that requires every housing development built in the wake of the 2012 Olympic Games to have one. While the lucky young residents of E15 and E20 currently have around a dozen to choose from (and more in the works), most kids would be overjoyed just to live close to this beauty with its epic play tower – a huge hardwood column filled with climbing ropes and several layers of net, and topped with a breathtaking tunnel slide that more than justifies all that clambering. Once the site of an old Olympic parking lot, this fully pedestrianised, pond-encircled plot is blissfully calm – save for the excited shrieks of children whizzing down that slide of course – and makes for a great post-shop stop-off, far from the clamour of Westfield.

NEARBY

Stratford Library has one of the best children's departments in the capital, offering diverse titles, craft classes and even its own Tube train.

DETAILS

Address: Forrester Way, E15 JLL

Station: Stratford International, Maryland

Barking Park

Sand, sailing and summertime splashing

If ever a green space was made for summer, it's this tranquil Victorian park. Home to a popular splash pad that opens from May, and a boating lake where families can rent unicorn-shaped pedalos outside of the winter months, the park also hosts an enticingly sandy playground whose elegant equipment appears to be sinking into the golden depths. While the latter is open year-round, it's best enjoyed when the sun's out, the sand is scattered with youngsters and the neighbouring cafe does a roaring trade in iced coffees and ice creams in a mind-boggling array of flavours. Equipment is best suited to younger kids, who'll delight in investigating the three-piece shipwreck with its lofty bird's nest and below-deck den, setting up home in the Wendy house village, and wriggling through the red hillside tunnel. Head here from late spring – and don't forget their buckets and spades.

NEARBY

Trampoline park chain Flip Out's largest London site is just a short bus ride away, while East London Gymnastics Centre offers incredible afternoon soft play sessions for under-5s, complete with gym equipment and a three-storey play structure.

DETAILS

Facilities: Toilets, baby change, cafe, picnic benches

Address: Longbridge Road, IG11 8TA

Station: Barking

Tumbling Bay

Natural play paradise in the Olympic Park

Forget Anish Kapoor's *Orbit*, this sprawling utopia is arguably the 2012 Olympic Games' greatest legacy, beloved by children across the capital and headlining many a tiny tourist's 'to do' list. Here, on the northern edge of the Queen Elizabeth Olympic Park, intrepid young explorers can scale nest-like climbing structures, tackle web-like rope canopies, cross rickety bridges and climb real trees, as well as explore an exceptionally elaborate system of dams, channels and splash pools, and the adjoining sandpit with its pulleys and chutes. Striking a balance between highly innovative and satisfyingly simple, Tumbling Bay will keep everyone from tiny tots to teens (and – let's face it – parents) entertained for hours, while the adjacent Timber Lodge Cafe will facilitate as many snack, toilet and (good) coffee breaks as you desire.

NEARBY

Take the kids swimming at the London Aquatics Centre and they'll never want to dip their toes in the local pool again. Coincide summertime visits with a cooling frolic in the 195-jet Waterworks Fountains or a relaxing cruise down the river in a swan pedalo.

DETAILS

Facilities: Toilets, baby change, cafe, picnic benches
Address: Olympic Park Avenue, E20 1DY
Station: Stratford International

Victoria Park Playgrounds

Fun, frolics and hair-raising hill slides

So-called because it once hosted a speakers' corner to rival Hyde Park's, the 'People's Park' is so well geared towards its child-encumbered visitors, it may as well call itself the Parent's Park. One of Britain's oldest public commons, this family favourite possesses not one, but two popular playgrounds, two child-friendly cafes, and a brilliant summertime splash pool. Both playgrounds have had several of their original wooden structures replaced by some profoundly ugly metal equipment – in particular the small ones' area at the western end of the park – though the larger of the two still impresses with its trio of breathtaking hillside slides, a bouncy bridge sandwiched between two rope climbing pyramids, and a series of musical jumping pads. Head here in the summer when the pedalos are on standby and the splash pool is babbling.

NEARBY

Grab lunch from playground-adjacent mum-run cafe The Hub, or proceed north to Victoria Park Village for bountiful coffee shops, family-friendly pubs (we recommend The Crown) and a browse around sustainable indie kids' store What Mother Made.

DETAILS

Facilities: Toilets, baby change, cafe, picnic benches
Address: E9 5DU
Station: Hackney Wick

Leyton Jubilee Park

Pirate fun in a swashbuckling playground

Seldom does a children's playground raise as many questions as this incongruous hodgepodge of structures. Why, for example, have almost all the slides been designed to be completely inaccessible to under-5s? And why are there so *many* slides? And yet, despite giving the impression of having been devised by a dozen different designers who've yet to meet, it still makes for a thoroughly enjoyable outing – provided you're tall enough to use it. The slides vary in design, though the majority spring from lofty, fort-like constructions, with yawning gaps between the entryways and platforms putting paid to toddler fun. The centrepiece – a huge, ship-shaped climbing frame – is much more tot-friendly, offering smalls a chance to climb the rigging, man the decks and maybe even walk the plank (or just jump ship via one of those slides).

NEARBY

Leyton offers no end of indie coffee shops, with favourites including SHED and Perky Blenders. Leyton Leisure Centre is a local institution, boasting three water slides, a giant flume and splash zone for 0–8s. And you can't leave the neighbourhood without a browse in Phlox Books.

DETAILS

Facilities: Toilets, baby change, cafe
Address: Seymour Road, E10 7BL
Station: Lea Bridge

Brunswick Park

Bijou green space with an independent cafe

Size-wise, this four-acre park might pale in comparison to its neighbour, the rambling Burgess Park, but don't let that deter you from dragging the gang here. For nestled among cool Camberwell's elegant Victorian villas you'll find one of south London's most family-friendly spaces; a leafy haven that's a parental saviour year-round thanks to its recently overhauled playground and adjoining Bower Hut Cafe – a coffee and cake kiosk so brilliant it should have an outpost in every playground in London. In terms of play, both tottering toddlers and fearless big kids are well catered for, with twin red and yellow wood structures (one a Wendy house plus tiny slide, the other a more precarious multi-access construction that encourages riskier play), as well as more standard equipment. Small? Sure. But that's unlikely to stop this gem from becoming a favourite.

NEARBY

South London Gallery is one of the capital's coolest art spaces, offering trailblazing exhibitions across two spectacular sites; a tranquil cafe serving Redemption Roasters coffee and moreish cakes and brunches; and monthly Sunday Spot workshops for 5–12s.

DETAILS

Facilities: Cafe, picnic benches
Address: Brunswick Park,
  SE5 7RJ
Station: Denmark Hill

Burgess Park

Natural playscape with treetop dens

With its towering natural play structures providing an experience akin to swinging (or fumbling) through the treetops, Burgess Park's newest play area is a significant departure from conventional playgrounds, offering a mentally and physically stimulating experience with the visuals to match. Built around a series of tree-like three-dimensional nests, or decagons, the playground invites adventurous children of all ages to play as they see fit – crawling through rope tunnels, scrambling up climbing nets, shooting down slides and firefighter's poles, and battling obstacles in whatever order they please, with absolutely no 'right' way to play. Away from the nests – or dodecahedrons as they're officially termed – little explorers will find swings for all ages and abilities, a sequence of balance beams and stepping poles, and tree-trunk benches for any adults whose assistance isn't required (though it's so pretty you might find yourself lending a hand regardless).

NEARBY

Fowlds does the best coffee in Camberwell and is just a one-minute walk away. Meanwhile, on the park's north side, a brightly coloured tarmac playscape offers a different sensory experience (plus cooling water jets in the summer months).

DETAILS

Facilities: Toilets, baby change, cafe, picnic benches
Address: Burgess Park, 40 New Church Road, SE5 7JJ
Station: Denmark Hill

Elephant Springs

The Rolls-Royce of splash pads

For the few short weeks every year when play fountains seem like the only place on Earth where you won't evaporate, a trip to Elephant Springs will make you think you've died and gone to heaven. Forming part of the new recreational space that rose from the ashes of the colossal, neo-Brutalist Heygate Estate, this summer-ready spot is constructed from 600 landscaped hunks of slip-resistant Italian stone that form the stage for an invigorating ensemble of motion-sensitive water jets, miniature waterfalls and babbling brooks, with gushing hand pumps and habitually damp slides upping the excitement. Surrounding this sparkling spectacle, a large sandpit, swinging rope hammocks and slab seating encourage all-day loafing, while a perfectly situated coffee kiosk should keep the grown-ups suitably caffeinated until home time.

NEARBY

If the temperature's high enough to warrant play fountains, you won't want to venture far. Luckily there's plenty to do in the immediate vicinity, from family-friendly sourdough pizza at Four Hundred Rabbits to an eclectic programme of free cultural events run by the park.

DETAILS

Facilities: Toilets, baby change, cafe, picnic benches
Address: Elephant Park, Elephant Road, SE17 1FR
Station: Elephant & Castle

Jubilee Gardens

Rambling riverside runabout

This permanently busy playground's popularity may be largely down to its tourist-trap location at the foot of the London Eye, but that's not to say it's not a good one anyway. Actually, it's a great one – a big, beguiling joy of a playground whose appeal has recently been given a serious boost with the addition of a ship-shaped structure with wonky gangways and below-deck dens. Elsewhere, the log assault course will appeal to kids well into their teens with its colossal climbing webs and lofty vantage points (the reward for all that clambering), while cute hidey houses and static animals cater to the opposite end of the age scale. Add in floor-mounted wobble boards, talking tubes and swinging boats, and you've got yourself one heck of a playground. Just remember not to blink – it's frighteningly easy to lose your kids in here.

NEARBY

The Southbank Centre offers weekly Rug Rhymes sessions, family shows and a cosy kids' reading area. Or, if you're looking for something more adult-friendly, Brewdog Waterloo has kids' meals, an in-house ice cream van and a massive slide (and beer, obviously).

DETAILS

Facilities: Toilets, baby change, cafe, picnic benches
Address: Belvedere Road, SE1 7PG
Station: Waterloo

Greenwich Park Playground

Seaside in the city

London's most breathtakingly beautiful park has a rich history of recreation, having hosted a children's playground on the same site since the 1940s, as well as being the one-time hunting ground of Henry VIII. Unsurprisingly, The Royal Parks didn't opt for a Tudor theme when revamping the play equipment (though Six Wives-shaped swings could have been fun). Instead, the design draws inspiration from the area's strong maritime connections, with a vast sand and water play area, and a smattering of boat-like structures. Accessibility is also a major consideration here, with wheelchair-friendly paths and roundabouts, accessible swings, wide slides, good sight lines and plenty of sensory elements, including scented plants and a focus on texture. Finally, an emphasis on collaborative play adds mettle to the nautical theme, with abundant opportunities for kids to work together as a crew. All hands on deck!

NEARBY

The Ahoy! indoor play zone at the National Maritime Museum offers more maritime-themed fun for 0–7s. Meanwhile, on the other side of the park, the Royal Observatory screens out-of-this-world planetarium shows for kids of all ages.

DETAILS

Facilities: Toilets, baby change, cafe, picnic benches
Address: SE10 8XG
Station: Maze Hill

Battersea Park Playground

Expansive play paradise for all ages

It's rare to find a playground so gargantuan that kids don't know where to begin, but it's a problem often encountered at Battersea Park's sprawling play metropolis. Technically several play areas clustered together, the site comprises a cute toddler zone with swings and ride-on vehicles; a more demanding area for juniors complete with climbing frames and a colourful slide tower; and a physically (and, at times, emotionally) challenging over-8s section whose structures are almost as lofty as the treetop walkways that encircle it – courtesy of the Go Ape outpost that shares the site (and which you'll need to purchase a ticket to have a swing on). Its brilliance means its packed on weekends and school holidays, while its size makes keeping tabs on the kids tricky – especially when they inevitably insist on running in opposite directions – so do yourself a favour and bring extra adults (and maybe even walkie-talkies).

NEARBY

The park has a brilliant children's zoo, pedalo-stocked boating lake and family-friendly lakeside cafe make a good case for staying all day. If you'd rather move on, head to Chelsea's iconic Saatchi Gallery or the National Army Museum's themed play space.

DETAILS

Facilities: Toilets, baby change, cafe, picnic benches
Address: SW11 4NJ
Station: Battersea Park

Cator Park North

Exhilarating ups and downs for courageous kids

Nestled among the foliage of Cator Park, a biodiverse green space established as part of the new Kidbrooke Village, this epic playscape may originally have been intended to serve the young residents, but its appeal extends far beyond the estate's boundary thanks to its wildly inventive design. Looping tunnel slides sprout from four-sided, branch-topped nests, making them resemble kites when viewed from above (or, at least, that's the idea) and earning the spot the nickname 'Kite Park'. On their own, these structures would make a playground worthy of a whole day's play, but they're just one part of this incredible space, which also hosts a bouldering wall, hillside slides, bridges and balance beams, along with dozens more climbing opportunities in various guises. It's not for the faint hearted, but older kids will delight in expanding their frontiers here.

NEARBY

Weather a bit iffy? Neighbouring Sutcliffe Park Sports Centre offers all-weather Clip 'n Climb with an adjoining soft-play frame. Or, if you're after a bit of culture, Eltham Palace provides family fun in a fascinating medieval-meets-Art Deco mansion.

DETAILS

Facilities: Toilets, baby change, cafe, picnic benches
Address: Kidbrooke Park Road, SE3 9JT
Station: Kidbrooke

The Magic Garden

Enchanting playground at Hampton Court

Magic comes alive at this bewitching playground, even if its mythical beasts have seemingly been turned to stone by a malevolent king. Speaking of which, entry is included when you buy a ticket to Henry VIII's most famous residence but you won't be able to visit the playground without one, so be sure to set aside a couple of hours to do it justice. Adults should start at the on-site kiosk, where they can grab coffee and cake before taking a pew and watching the fairy-tale fun unfold. The kids, meanwhile, probably won't know where to start, but a game of hide and seek should quickly acquaint them with this enchanting space, which incorporates treetop walks, stately towers, concealed lairs, a king-sized water-play area and – the *pièce de résistance* – a gargantuan ruby-eyed dragon, all in lusciously leafy surroundings.

NEARBY

You'll need a whole day to explore the Tudor palace and its numerous delights, which include a famously perplexing 300-year-old maze and lively programme of family-friendly events.

DETAILS

Facilities: Toilets, baby change, cafe, picnic benches
Address: KT8 9AU
Station: East Molesey

Hobbledown Heath

Kids' steampunk-style metropolis

Said to be London's biggest indoor and outdoor adventure playground, this Hobbiton-esque amusement park packs in so many play structures it's borderline ridiculous – though at least the substantial admission fee is (just about) justified. Fun for all ages but particularly well suited to older kids, Hobbledown's second instalment is more than twice the size of its Epsom sister-site, offering not one, but *four* thrilling fantasy play areas designed to pique their imaginations, test their scrambling skills and fuel some serious fun. Taking the form of 'villages', each play area has its own unique character, from the madcap Cribble Creek with its twisting chutes, slides and wheels to the bustling Buckbridge Market with its role play-ready shops. Add in aerial adventures, an epic indoor Play Barn and even an on-site zoo, and it might be worth investing in annual membership.

NEARBY

Sister-site Gripped offers discounted add-on tickets when you buy admission to Hobbledown. Here, plucky adventurers can take on perilous high ropes, extreme speed slides, exhilarating zip wires and nail-biting bag jumps – if they dare.

DETAILS

Facilities: Toilets, baby change, cafe, picnic benches
Address: Staines Road, TW14 0HH
Station: Feltham, Hounslow West

Prospect Place

Powerfully good playtime

It might stand in the vast shadow of Battersea's iconic power station, but this shiny new playground is no shrinking violet. In fact, violet is just one of the many colours in its kaleidoscopic palette. Built around a towering quartet of play towers, from which rope bridges, twisting tube slides and spiral staircases shoot, this eye-popping playscape packs a powerful punch in spite of its modest footprint, providing hours of playtime in an exceptionally striking package. Ideal for all ages, its structures manage to be accessible to younger children while still posing challenges for older ones, with access options ranging from easy-access steps to treacherous rope ladders. Balance equipment, bucket swings and a tilting roundabout complete the play offer, while the undulating rainbow hillscape provides endless scope for Floor-is-Lava-style shenanigans.

NEARBY

There's loads of family fun to be had on the Battersea Power Station estate, from mini golf at Birdies to kid-friendly dining at Megan's, Tonkotsu and Where the Pancakes Are, plus regular parent-and-baby classes and family events.

DETAILS

Facilities: Toilets, baby change, cafe, picnic benches
Address: Circus Road West, SW8 5BN
Station: Battersea Power Station

Canons Playground

Topsy-turvy timber playscape

It's no surprise that this creative playground was co-designed by children (though it is surprising that children aren't always involved in playground design when the results look like this). Located in the grounds of the historic Canons House – and next to a rather less historic leisure centre – this stimulating space draws inspiration from the site's medieval dovecote, with two of its primary structures reimagining the building as a series of versatile multi-use dens. Elsewhere, an ingenious mountain of timber folds takes its design cues from the kids' experiments with scrunched-up paper, and can be clambered on or crawled beneath, with openings facilitating movement between the two levels. A play on gradient adds to the sense of fun, with tilted forms creating the illusion of a dizzying parallel universe where everything is delightfully off-kilter.

NEARBY

The neighbouring leisure centre runs Aqua Splash inflatable assault course sessions for over–8s on weekends – and has an elephant-shaped pool slide. Slightly further afield, head to Morden Hall Park for family fun and Deen City Farm for pony rides.

DETAILS

Facilities: Toilets, baby change, cafe, picnic benches
Address: Canons Leisure Centre, Madeira Road, CR4 4HD
Station: Mitcham Junction

Peckham Rye Playground

Soaring structures and watery fun

Whether they're 15 or 1.5, kids are sure to find their thing at this bold and beautiful playground. Located slap bang in the centre of Peckham Rye Park and Common, this spacious site is dominated by an impressive water-play landscape crafted from natural stone, and features cascading streams, retractable dams and easy-to-activate water pumps designed for little hands – though popular with all ages come the warmer months. At the far end of the space, a spectacular, if rather unnerving, arrangement of wooden stilts, wobbly bridges and near-vertical slides caters to the park's longer-limbed visitors, being accessible exclusively via a rickety climbing net or perilous tightrope walkway. Plentiful swings and a series of sand-dipped wooden play-houses equipped with compact slides seal the deal, while ample adult seating and proximity to the park cafe ensure it's an all-day affair.

NEARBY

The adjacent Round cafe serves delicious single-origin coffee. Apple Tree Cafe is south London's ultimate 0–5s destination with its sensory room and soft-play frame, while Peckham Levels' colourful play area offers an unconventional rainy-day option.

DETAILS

Facilities: Toilets, baby change, cafe, picnic benches
Address: Peckham Rye Common, SE15 3UA
Station: Nunhead

Brockwell Park Playground

Water, wood and miniature train rides

Wood seems to be the overarching theme of Brockwell Park's sprawling playscape, and while that might not sound particularly unique or adventurous, it somehow accomplishes both. A proper destination playground, it offers both an eclectic choice of equipment and a broad appeal across age groups, which accounts for its often-overwhelming busyness on fair-weather days. Inhabitable play structures of varying shapes and sizes pepper the site, from small playhouses to larger forts and huge log hangouts, creating a village-like design that inspires collaborative play across the entire space. Sizzling days call for an invigorating splash in the park's wet-play area – a heaven-sent combination of rocky splash pond and capacious paddling pool – while, on the other side on the park, the miniature railway tootles between Herne Hill Gate and Brockwell Lido on Sundays from March to October.

NEARBY

Favourites on the park's Herne Hill side include kids' bookshop Tales on Moon Lane, sustainable womenswear store Lowie and station coffee spot Arcade. Or head north to Brixton Village for endless lunch options and diverse books from Round Table.

DETAILS

Facilities: Toilets, baby change, cafe, picnic benches
Address: Brockwell Park, SW2 2ST
Station: Herne Hill

Dexters Adventure Playground

Timber fun house on a significant site

Though sparse in terms of its loose parts, this modest plot is home to one of the most breathtaking fixed structures we've found in an adventure playground. Designed by Erect Architecture, the team responsible for dozens of the capital's most creative open-access playgrounds, this glorious tangle of wood draws inspiration from houses on the street that were destroyed in the Brixton Riots, with playable domestic elements including sloped planks that mimic bannisters, drainpipe ladders to scale, and cosy attic spaces that look out across the neighbourhood. On Saturdays, kids of all ages are invited to explore the playground and colourful games pitch, while a youth club for teens and pre-teens runs after school and in the holidays – a testament to its versatility. That said, you might want to give this one a miss with smaller kids on rainy days, when wet surfaces quickly transform the structure from fun to petrifying.

NEARBY

Neighbouring Koala Coffee is perfect for pre-play lattes (or post-play ice creams). Brixton Village favourite Round Table Books specialises in inclusive kids' titles, while Slime Planet stages gorgeously gooey interactive workshops at its Loughborough Junction studio.

DETAILS

Facilities: Toilets
Address: 6 Montego Close, SE24 0LH
Station: Brixton

Clapham Park Estate

Old-school fun in a Brutalist folly

London's oldest surviving play structure still packs a punch more than half a century after it was produced – thanks to some clever engineering and a solid commitment to maintenance. Built to serve the kids of Clapham Park West Estate in 1969, this Brutalist creation might at first seem uninspiring with its grey concrete shell and stark spiral form, but it's this non-prescriptive design that makes it so appealing – and probably one of the reasons why it's survived this long. With its gentle slope, the meandering slide is as much fun to scramble up as it is to slither down, while its tubular tunnels make excellent dens and reading nooks, and the tiled dome begs to be scaled. Adults, meanwhile, can survey the action from one of the built-in benches – or relive their youth with a go on that slide.

NEARBY

Studio Voltaire hosts groundbreaking art exhibitions in a captivating space with a great cafe. Around the corner in Brixton, Substation bouldering centre provides a kids-only climbing room, while Round Table Books specialises in inclusive kids' titles.

DETAILS

Address: Belgravia House, Clarence Avenue, SW4 8HY
Station: Clapham Common

Brunel Estate

Catch a riotous ride on a seventies slide

Not many playgrounds can lay claim to a Grade II-listed slide, but then not many slides make it into their fifth (nearly sixth) decade. Laid out during the construction of Westbourne Park's Brunel Estate in 1973, this modernist masterpiece consists of a long sliver of metal cascading through a colossal, bespoke climbing structure made entirely from red brick. Originally featuring a series of footholds and open handrails to swing past, the slide has been lightly modified in recent years, with metal fences introduced to bring it more in line with modern safety standards (though, if anything, they've simply presented new hazards). The equipment that sits alongside the large slide is pretty standard issue, but who cares when you've got this beauty to bolt down?

NEARBY

Museum of Brands is surprisingly great for kids, offering themed family trails and a chance for the adults to indulge in a bit (okay, a lot) of nostalgia. Older ones will go batty for BAYSIXTY6, a spectacular skate park nestled beneath the Westway.

DETAILS

Address: Westbourne Park Road, W2 5UZ
Station: Royal Oak

The Children's Garden

Plant-themed play in Kew Gardens

'What do plants need to grow?' ponder the stepping-stones that line the path leading to this awe-inspiring space. Kids needn't look far to find the answers – they're right there in the form of four distinct play zones, each one themed around the needs in question. The Earth Zone is all about worming through tube slides and digging in the sand, while the Air Zone will appeal to smaller ones with its giant 'pollen' spheres and mini trampolines. The Water Zone is self-explanatory, made up of paddling ponds and rockpools, while the Sun Zone functions as a chillout space with its large lawn and glowing sun tunnel. It's exquisitely done, right down to the 4m-high canopy walk – a mini version of Kew's celebrated treetop walkway. The only downside? You need to purchase a ticket to the Gardens to use the playground.

NEARBY

There's more than enough across Kew's 500-acre site to fill a day (or 10). Highlights include the buzzing Hive installation and Victorian Palm House. Peckish? Head to the fantasy-themed Family Kitchen for stone-baked pizza and eye-popping ice cream.

DETAILS

Facilities: Toilets, baby change, cafe, picnic benches
Address: TW9 3AE
Station: Kew Gardens

Paddington Recreation Ground

Showstopping space with a storybook theme

Paddington Bear references abound at what is arguably the capital's most inventive play space, despite most being so subtle you'll likely miss them (and the fact that the park they reside in isn't technically in Paddington). In the toddler area, a row of pastel-hued townhouses recalls the Brown family's fictional Windsor Gardens home and conceals a vertical wooden maze, while the adorable railway station and play train reference their charge's arrival in London. Over in the junior area, a stunner of a steamboat alludes to Paddington's voyage to England from darkest Peru, linking up to a bridge that connects the playground's two halves. The towering treetop structure and zip wire are designed to test big kids and teens, while the stimulating sensory trail targets neurodiverse visitors with its plants, flowers and musical instruments (plus a suitcase-toting bear sculpture that's tantalisingly touchable and unmistakably Paddington).

NEARBY

The park cafe makes a mean latte and sells ice creams in the summer. The delights of Little Venice are just a short walk away – and the Puppet Barge Theatre's magical marionette performances are a particular hit with families.

DETAILS

Facilities: Toilets, baby change, cafe, picnic benches
Address: Randolph Avenue, W9 1PF
Station: Maida Vale

Holland Park

Challenging play with a zooming zip wire

Is it any coincidence that possibly the capital's best-looking park contains what is likely its best-looking playground? And, far from being just a pretty face, it offers what might be its most exciting play experience, too. Designated for ages five and up, this gorgeously landscaped, imaginatively designed wonderland allows kids of all ages and abilities to let loose and push their physical boundaries, whether they're scaling the soaring Fishing Tower's network of ropes, navigating the swirling Hillcoaster's sloping walkway, hitching a ride on the communal dragon swing or braving what might be the most forceful zip wire we've ever encountered. Sound a bit too intense for your little one? The sand-sunken toddler area offers an easygoing alternative at the other end of the park.

NEARBY

The Design Museum's free exhibits and gift shop are always worth a browse, even if its paid exhibitions aren't always child-friendly. Kids' boutiques Hop Like a Bunny and Mini Rodini are great for gifts – and usually worth the expense.

DETAILS

Facilities: Toilets, baby change, cafe, picnic benches
Address: 55 Abbotsbury Road, W14 8EL
Station: Holland Park, Kensington (Olympia)

Fitzrovia Children's Play Area

Secret playground for weekend fun

Despite sitting in the shadow of one of London's most easily recognisable buildings (yep, the big BT tower), remarkably few people seem to be aware of this clandestine playground's existence. Closed to the public on term-time weekdays owing to its use by the neighbouring nursery – something that's only advertised via the tiny sign on its unassuming gate – the space is, somewhat surprisingly, best suited to school-age kids (specifically 8–12s), who are welcome to swing by on weekends and holidays. Apparatus is on the scarce side, with a towering treehouse (reachable only via a minimalist rope ladder or very precarious walkway) and an expansive climbing wall making up the bulk of the play offer. Much more than the sum of its parts, the playground is unique in providing space for older children to safely indulge in risky play, slap bang in the heart of the city.

NEARBY

Museums! Choose from the Wellcome Collection, Grant Museum of Zoology, British Museum, Charles Dickens Museum, Foundling Museum and more. Provided you're sans-buggy, head to Attendant for great coffee in a Victorian former public toilet.

DETAILS

Address: 54a Whitfield Street, WIT 4ER
Station: Goodge Street

Diana Memorial Playground

Finding Neverland in Kensington

If you only visit one London playground, this Peter Pan-themed paradise should probably be it. Dedicated to the late Princess of Wales and located close to her former home in the lush surrounds of Kensington Gardens, this sandy playscape feels every inch the otherworldly wonderland with its exotic trees, remarkably realistic Jolly Roger and an outer wall that serves to block out the surrounding landscape, creating a truly immersive environment in which to lose yourself (and not your child). And while the aforementioned Jolly Roger might be the star of the show with its captain's cabin, climbable crow's nest and below-deck hideout, the fun definitely doesn't stop there, with summer-ready sand and water play, Lost Boys-inspired treehouses and loads more to explore around the 'island'. Bring a picnic and stay all day – there's even an on-site toilet so you never (never) have to leave.

NEARBY

Swerve the exorbitant park kiosk and get your fix from Kensington's Lift Coffee instead. Kensington Palace offers a child-friendly glimpse into the early life of Queen Victoria, and the dynamic Diana Memorial Fountain is a sacred spot in the summer months.

DETAILS

Facilities: Toilets, baby change, cafe, picnic benches
Address: Kensington Gardens, Broad Walk, W2 4RU
Station: Queensway

Northala Fields

Fantasy fun in a manmade hillscape

It might sound (and look) like something out of *The Chronicles of Narnia*, but this fantasy playscape can be found just off the A40 (and not at the back of a wardrobe). Located at the foot of the park's four artificial mounds, which were summoned from the rubble of the old Wembley Stadium, the playground takes the form of a single, sprawling playframe constructed almost entirely from golden timber logs. Different levels cater to different age groups and are connected by a labyrinthine network of ladders and bridges of varying levels of precariousness. Meanwhile, the hillside setting presents its own challenges, particularly in wet weather, while also upping the thrill factor of the structure's lengthy slides. There's not loads to tempt tiny ones here, but the colourful, mix-and-match spinning panels should keep them occupied long enough for the big kids to do a few laps.

NEARBY

Take on the Horsenden Hill Gruffalo Trail and hunt down giant sculptural versions of the book's characters, or head to Hanwell Zoo in search of miniature donkeys, lemurs, margays and capybaras.

DETAILS

Facilities: Toilets, cafe, picnic benches
Address: Westway Close, UB5 6UR
Station: Northolt

Image credits

Photography by *Martin Usborne* except for the images listed below:

Barking Park (second image) ©Robin Forster Photography / LDA Design; Tumbling Bay, Architecture & Play Design: Erect Architecture, Photography: David Grandorge; Brunel Estate ©Jack Young; Canons Playground ©Studio Hardie; Cator Park North ©Simon Winson / Berkeley Group; Clapham Park Estate ©Emmy Watts; Claremont Park ©Duncan & Grove; Dexters Adventure Playground ©Dellali Defor, Bigkid Foundation; Diana Memorial Playground (first image) ©Peter Phipp/Travelshots.com / Alamy Stock Photo; Elephant Springs ©John Sturrock / Gillespies; Forrester Way ©Duncan & Grove; Gloucester Gate (second and third images) ©Duncan & Grove; Golden Lane Estate ©Taran Wilkhu; Greenwich Park Playground ©The Royal Parks; Hobbledown Heath (first and second images) ©Paul Taylor; Hobbledown Heath (third and fourth images) ©Oliver Dixon; Holland Park Playground, Landscape & Play Design: Erect Architecture, Photography: Henrietta Williams; Marylebone Green ©PA Images / Alamy Stock Photo; Northala Fields (first image) ©The Children's Playground; Northala Fields (second image) @markoandplacemakers; Royal Air Force Museum ©RAF Museum; Somerford Grove Adventure Playground ©Emmy Watts; Wood Wharf Play Space, Marvellous Maze, Play Design: Erect Archiecture, Photography: Henrietta Williams; The Children's Garden (first image), by Charlie J Ercilla / Alamy Stock Photo; The Children's Garden (third and fourth images) ©Duncan & Grove; Parsloes Park ©Thierry Bal; The Magic Garden (second image) ©Historic Royal Palaces; The Magic Garden (third image) ©Historic Royal Palaces / David Hedges; Burgess Park ©Duncan & Grove.

London's Best Playgrounds
First edition

Published in 2023 by Hoxton Mini Press, London
Copyright © Hoxton Mini Press 2023. All rights reserved.

Text by Emmy Watts
All photography by Martin Usborne*
Copy-editing by Octavia Stocker
Proofreading by Gaynor Sermon
Additional design by Richard Mason
Production by Sarah-Louise Deazley
Production and editorial support by Georgia Williams

*Except for additional images credited on previous page.

With thanks to Matthew Young for help developing the series design.

A CIP catalogue record for this book is available from the British Library.

ISBN: 978-1-914314-37-7

Printed and bound by Finidr, Czech Republic

Hoxton Mini Press is an environmentally conscious publisher, committed
to offsetting our carbon footprint. This book is 100 per cent carbon compensated,
with offset purchased from Stand For Trees.

For every book you buy from our website, we plant a tree:
www.hoxtonminipress.com